Rise

Reclamation

BLUE FORGE PRESS

Port Orchard ✹ Washington

Blue Forge Press is the print division of the volunteer-run, federal 501 (c)3 nonprofit company, Blue Forge Group, founded in 1989 and dedicated to bringing light to the shadows and voice to the silence. We strive to empower storytellers across all walks of life with our four divisions: Blue Forge Press, Blue Forge Films, Blue Forge Gaming, and Blue Forge Records. Find out more at www.BlueForgeGroup.org

Blue Forge Press
7419 Ebbert Drive Southeast
Port Orchard, Washington 98367
blueforgepress@gmail.com
360-550-2071 ph.txt

To every woman who has been told
to be quiet, small, or forgetful of her power—
we offer this chorus.
May your voice return in full,
louder and lovelier than ever before.
Reclamation is a holy act,
and these poems are its prayer.

Table of Contents

Reclamation

Michelle

Lee

Rope

We are connected
by an invisible rope—
one end tied around your waist,
the other end
around my chest.
When you teeter on the edge,
I get pulled down with you.
When I wander,
seeking solace,
you tug hard
and yank me back;
as if you fear I'll see something
more desirable.
Or an escape.
When I fall,
you circle me;
and that rope winds around my neck,
choking my airways,
taking me to the brink
of insanity or death.
It's a constant game
of tug a war,
and I'm scared what will happen

when one day,
you pull too hard and the rope snaps,
and the sweet taste of freedom
kisses our lips.
Will the world shatter,
or only us?
As the fragments of everything
rain down over our heads
like broken promises,
dreams lost to the ether.
Because without that rope
what holds us together?

Strangers

We are familiar strangers,
dancing in the night
around each other.
Close enough to touch,
yet no fingers encounter flesh.
We are familiar strangers,
going through the motions
that once drove us
into each other's arms.
We search for the words
to bring those feelings back,
yet, we fall short
and rebound with small talk
that neither of us cares about.
When did we go separate ways
and talk to each other
across an open field of land mines?
From roads that sometimes
ran parallel to each other
but more often curved away?
We are familiar strangers,
and every day, I wonder
if I can find my way to you,

and if you would even welcome me.
Because I feel like it's my fault
that we drifted.
Because life grew challenging,
and I went into survival mode,
forgetting that I had someone
to lean on.
And that was the beginning
of becoming familiar strangers.
Of me becoming angry
instead of facing the emotions
burning me alive.
I didn't face the shame
that ate at me because
I couldn't provide more;
that I wasn't who I should be.
Fear that I won't be enough,
that my choices are wrong.
Embarrassed that I was weak.
So I allowed anger to be the wedge;
and now we are familiar strangers.

After

I hear all the time
about happily ever after.
What no one speaks of
is everything after happy...
the pull to succeed
even while failing;
the losing yourself
in the grab for the illusion
of what you want others to see.
No one tells you
that after happy
comes all the other emotions
that test the strength of your soul:
the pain, anger, fear
so desperately hidden from view
lest the accusations begin
that life isn't happy.
It's only after everything,
that you learn
happily ever after
means after happy
comes the growth.

It's messy,
terrifying,
awful;
and hard to learn
that chasing happily ever after
never stops.
To keep it means
always fighting,
forgiving,
and learning
that after happy is an
obstacle course.

Survivor

You say I'm strong
like it's a good thing;
 that everything that destroyed my life
 is something to be celebrated.
I don't agree.

Strength is an illusion, a façade,
 a pretty word to dress up trauma dealt by the
hands of others.

You say I'm strong,
 believing I should be proud
  that I'm still standing.
But you forget that wasn't always the case.
I had to learn to stand and walk again.

You tell me I'm strong,
 as though it should give me confidence
  when everything I do
   tells you *that* doesn't exist for me.
It was taken from me and I need to find it again.

Don't tell me I'm strong.
It's a discredit to the skills I've built;
  how I tore myself apart and taught myself
   to keep going, to live, to rebuild.
The skills I've honed and crafted,
  with each transgression aimed to topple me.

Don't say I'm strong.
Choose better words to honor me.
  Tell me I'm powerful.
   A fighter not to be trifled with
    for the entertainment of those who
  see me as less.
Say there is no force greater than the steel of my spine,
  when malicious winds from mouths of evil
   try to bend me to their will.

Don't undermine me
  with the phrase 'you are strong',
   simply because I suffered the perils of men
  with low self-esteem and power complexes.

I want to be seen for more. I am more.

I'm not strong.
I'm human, an apex predator in my own right,
  and I was born to survive.

Jonielle
McMurtrey

Piano

I never knew
How much my life
Was spent
Near
Listening to
Touching
A piano

One day
I realized
It's been years
Since I heard fingers
Flying across a piano

My dream
Was to one day play
With grace and precision
Alas
My tiny fingers
Struggled with ebony and ivory

I long to hear your fingers flying across the keys

I want to be taken back in time
To a time
Where life had no responsibilities
But to be home by dark
Where I could run free
And be graced by the arms of love

I sit now
At a piano
And I wish
Just once
I could hear you play
From dawn until dusk
Fill my ears with your passion
Make the wooden piece of furniture
Pieced together with wires and ebony and ivory
And make the entire room fill with your magic
As your fingers glide
So effortlessly
Across the keys

Take me back in time
Give me the technology I have today
So, I can record you
Playing
Over and over again

And play it back on the days we're missing you
Seems unbearable
And to remind me of your love
Grace
And joy

I sit now
And stare at the keys
Ebony and ivory
How did you make them sing so effortlessly
How did you make it come to life
With just a touch of your hands

Come sit beside me
Make music to my ears once again
Let me hold onto that moment

Let the piano
Free my soul

Woman

Woman
What a word
So much meaning
So complex
A woman
A mom
A sister
A lover
A friend
A wife
A daughter

Each role
Has its own meaning
Demands
Yet
The woman shows up
Every day
Whether she wants to
Or not
Because
As a woman
That is what we do

Long ago
The roles weren't that different
Except
Women had to hide
Be the woman the man wanted
And if they dared to be different
Independent
They were ridiculed

Today
Woman
Has come to mean so much more
For now
We are recognizing
Our roles
Our true value

Mother
Daughter
Sister
Lover
Dominant
Aunt
Queen
Princess

You choose the name
You choose the role

Compassion
Love
Joy
Loyalty

We give it all
We are it all

Years ago, we couldn't be anything
Without the man's permission

Today
We are the heart and soul of life

Tell me
Who else could hold the power
To bring new life into this world
Besides a woman

We keep giving life
To this dying world
In hopes
Some day

Our power
Our love
Our patience
Our perseverance
Will be a message to all

Not all
Can give the breath of life
Except
A woman

Beautiful Woman

I see you there
your silver hair
your face covered in wrinkles
your skin
loose and thin
with age spots
sun, wind damaged
and the face
you no longer recognize
staring back at you

I see you

The life you've lived
The changes you've seen
You came from a world
where being a woman
only meant
the woman belongs inside her house
—making it a home
and nothing else
Now
being a woman

means the sky is the limit
There is nothing you can't do

I see you

What do you feel
when you see
the world has accepted
a woman can be a president
What do you see
when you open your door
to the outside world
and see women
running a home
a business
a family
all the while
owning her own name
and never giving someone power over her
because it's no longer
a part of the world

I see you
I feel you
The past
The present
The future

You age
as life becomes timeless.
Making your past
a time
women in the future
will never know

A time before cars
A time before cell phones
A time before computers
A time our children will never know existed
if it wasn't for you

I see you
with your silver hair
your face
wrinkled from smiles, tears, and the unknown
beautiful as ever
Your skin
that felt a life of youth and adventures

Beautiful woman
I see you

I Would've Let You Borrow Some of My Light

It's hard living today
In a time where there are so many
Different avenues for help
Yet, the feeling of being alone
It is stronger than ever

Afraid to love
Afraid to be free
Always guarded
For the first wrong interpretation
Of your actions
Or your words
Can have a tsunami effect
Taking the life you knew
And making it into
A mere memory

I've been there
I lived that
And I would've let you borrow my light

Your smile
Your gift to each
Your ability to make a body feel new
Gone
Because you didn't ask
To borrow some of my light
Which would've helped your own light grow
And shine through the cracks of your broken soul

Now
You are a part of the void

I've been there
I've lived that
I would've let you borrow some of my light

When it all seems too dark
And the world is heavy on your shoulders
Share the load
Friend
Sister
A bond made of love
Will always
Let you borrow some of their light
Until you can find your own again

You are never alone
You will always have someone
Who wants to hear your tears
Fears
Instead of holding the hands of your loved ones
Because they don't understand
What pain was so unbearable
So heavy
You couldn't let others in
To lighten the load

I would've let you borrow some of my light

You would've known
You weren't alone in your pain
Your struggles
You would've been able
To borrow just enough light
To spark your own and remember
This life is worth fighting for

Don't crawl into a dark corner to hide
Don't let this world destroy you
And if you feel it's becoming too much
And you can't see through the darkness

Reach out

Borrow some of my light
Before the darkness
Borrows your soul forever
For darkness
Doesn't deserve
To feel your love
You're scared to let through the cracks

You will feel my light
Fill the darkness surrounding you
And give you the piece of light
You have been searching for
To spark your own light back into existence

I would've given you the light you needed
For the world tried to give me darkness

I gave it light

Look at Us Now

When we were kids
Not a care in the world
The worries didn't exist
And our dreams
Were just a dream away

We grew up
We became moms
And aunts
And we did it!

We shook the traumas of the past free
We took their words of hate
And wore them proudly with love
We took their words of anger,
And returned east slap
With an iron will that couldn't be broken
And we set ourselves free!

Taking control
Of us
Who we are
Who we want to be

Loving the road it's taken to get there
While remaining humble to life's lessons
Our grandparents
Are, or would be
Proud of the women we are today.

It's not easy
To go from what we've known
To what we are today
Especially, in today's world
Where one wrong word
Can turn your kindness
Into something unknown

We know our worth
We know the love we give
Can be matched
If we are patient
And don't settle for less
Than what we deserve

Look at us now

Free

Warriors Made from Time

We live in a time now
Where the wrong words
Have catastrophic consequences
Where people feel more alone
Than they ever have before
Yet, we have more forms of communication
Than ever before

Yet
When you see another woman hurting
Being hurt
Being shamed
Whether she's a stranger or a loved one
You become her
Warrior made from time.

There's no more fear
There's a warrior made from time

Ready to battle
To fight a fight

Generations to generations
Change after change
One thing has always remained unchanged

Women
Big
Small
Tall
Short
Cury
Every type
Will always
Set fear aside
When another woman is being hurt

And become
Her warrior made from time

Bree

Indigo

Ocean Eternal

when I was five
the ocean was small
just like me
a tiny stretch of shoreline
in Snohomish County
beside the train tracks
you already loved
(and fifteen years before
we fell in love)

a few years later
my grandmother drove me
to the Pacific Ocean
all the way to the coast
not the rocky, rugged beach
full of sea stacks
secret caves and coves
but to the Baja California Peninsula
and a long stretch of
fine, mica-gilded sand
and warm waters I swam in
alone

she would bring me to this coast again
thirteen years old, and this time
we were at the aptly named Long Beach
flat and sandy like Ensenada
but in the state we call our home
with cooler waters I still loved
my feet pulling me toward the tideline
shoes or sandals discarded
to wade or swim
in any season

but much like the first time
your ocean eyes caught
my forested gaze
my heart has belonged
to the Northwest edge
of our Washington coastline
since the very first time
you brought me to La Push
and I set eyes on the faded denim
blues and grays
of her sand, stones, and seas
stallions charging in the wild waves
as if Arwen Undomiel
commanded them herself

I am eternally grateful
for the gift of that trip
the countless one since
and the incredible love
I feel for this place
for our home
for our children
and our beautiful life
for you and your heart
and all the immeasurable
gifts you have given
and shared with me
my heart and soul tied to yours
in this life and the next
as our twenty-one grams of stardust
flickers through the universe
together

This is Just to Say

the air was warm, not yet hot
when I stepped out of our room
into the dappled sunlight
under the canopy of cherry trees
planted when you claimed
this land as your own
and crossed to the newest
we planted last year
and this is just to say

I have eaten
the first cherry
that grew from
her branches

and which
you were probably
saving
for later

forgive me
she was delicious
so sweet
and so ripe

Green Thumb

the sun peeks through
the cherry tree leaves
stretching above me
like the lens flares
in your film

I sway in my hammock
in the hot July breeze
an ache in my chest
where my heart should be
but it leaves with you
as you pull out of our driveway
the sound of tires in gravel fading

robins and squirrels squabble
over sun-ripened cherries
grown from the trees you planted
a quarter-century ago
before you planted and grew
the children I now cherish and love
as if I had planted them
myself

when I feel ungrounded
and adrift, lost
in a tempestuous sea
of life's currents and tides
gusts blowing in all four directions
fate and choice, oaths and secrets
disorienting the truths I know
and confusing my compass
I close my eyes
and find this place
a piece of peace
grown in the fertile garden
of your making
cultivated by the hands
I know better than my own
which have cared for me
just as carefully
tending my heart and mind
mending the damage left by others
who came before, who didn't have
your green thumb or gentle touch
who could never know
every piece of me
every inch of me
the way you do

Thunder Moon

the new moon rose in Cancer
above our personal sky last night
leaving the stars illuminated
like a handful of quartz and mica
thrown across the night sky
and leaving my Capricorn moon
adrift and untethered
(or maybe I'm just another
new age hippie millennial
blaming the moon
for my own dysfunction)

it reminds me of the night
of our daughter's sixteenth birthday
I stood on the back deck
our cabin dark and quiet
looking up over the Pacific Ocean
and gazed at more stars
than I've ever seen in my life
never before
and never since

in these quiet moments
when time itself
and even the
high-speed ricocheting
thoughts of my mind
seem to still
it is here
in these moments
whether you're fifteen feet away
waiting in bed for me
or fifty miles away
on our Olympic peninsula
that I can feel you
with me
always

Cardamom Tesseract

I am standing in our kitchen
dicing apples that grew
just outside our bedroom windows
our first true harvest
in at least sixteen years
the cauldron boils
spices fill the air
before the apples
even begin to cook
cinnamon, nutmeg, cloves
ginger and cardamom
and I pause, lifting the small jar
to inhale and I am knocked
off my feet and into
autumn of 2008
and I am there with you
as you are here with me
in august and everything after

Bonsai

you walk beside me
in your cable knit sweater
grey like the overcast
late-autumn sky
tight auburn ringlets
streaked with fine strands of silver
tucked under your
black cabbie hat
and I think to myself
how you look like
a lighthousekeeper of yesteryear
though I bet you'd rather
be a train conductor
on the BNSF
you love so much

every year
the county trims
all the plants
weeds, shrubs, and trees
the rotary saw tearing
through anything
in its path

all along the roadside
over the drainage ditches
and around the power lines

and still, some plants
survive the carnage
broken and splintered
forever changed
by the violence
they've endured
sending out new growth
blindly, despite
—or perhaps
in spite

your eyes, blue denim
like the Levi's you wear
don't see destruction
your hands reach down
gently unbury her roots
fingertips carefully cradling
frayed branches
finding beauty
(your hands)
reached down
gently unburied

her roots
fingertips carefully cradling
frayed branches
finding beauty
in her mangled form
and strength in
her resilience
with a firm but tender tug
she comes free
under your touch

broken, ripped, and frayed
by time and the machine
that is our post-industrial capitalist life
lying in the ditch
unvalued and abandoned
you saw the promise
of her potential
and found, not a weed
but a bonsai

Ten Thousand and Eighty

we once watched
an episode of Bones
where the victim was so much
like Temperance
that she thought she was
seeing her own corpse
and it took three days
for her brain to adjust
and finally
see the truth

for three nights
I fell asleep
my eyes closed
feeling your gentle presence
behind me
and for three mornings
I woke with tears
down my cheek
soaking my pillow
because you weren't
beside me

but... I adjust

now I wake
in our quiet house
and I spend my day
seeing to the needs
of the gentle creatures
who live in our home
and my pillow is dry
until I fall into exhaustion
sometime near the dawn
(if even at all)
unable any longer
to distract myself
from you

it's one week
ten thousand eighty
minutes too long
of fleeting moments
in stolen kisses, a quick embrace
poems and voice memos
cartoons and notes
folded and so high school
just one week
of this pang in my chest

but the tiger lilies have opened
a riotous symphony of
sunset hues
new poppies have grown
shading the scattered crimson petals
of the last bloom
and I pace outside
in circles at night
treading concrete and dirt paths
moss and overgrown cobblestones
treading but sinking
because I hate that I know
how it feels to be here
with you gone
and I hate that I know
that I can wake without tears
alone in our bed
and I hate that I know
that I can live our life
in our home, with our kids
and how both the
mundane and extraordinary
continue
without you

and the heart-shaped box
in my chest overflows
with the unspoken truth
I have always held:
one day
I will walk our land
without you

and despite my jokes
about bad genetics
I have seen my parents
survive what they shouldn't
after a lifetime spent
in temples of self-neglect
while I reparent myself
healing and growing
a decade spent
finding my health
and while nothing is certain
(because cancer or bears
an aneurysm or drunk driver
can happen to anyone)
the math doesn't lie

I can't count them yet
but I know there will be

too many weeks
without you
pacing our land in circles
lost in memory
and a lifetime of love
a ghost of my own making
under your cherry trees
and beneath our personal sky

and yet...
I see you everywhere
sweet peas growing wild
around every corner
anywhere I drive
our front planter, full of weeds
suddenly half-full of poppies
(but only after you
sent me your poem)
and incredulous joy
swells in me
as I drop to my knees
before this offering
pulling sow thistles
and creeping buttercup
so they don't
choke your garden

and I laugh as I see
first a ladybug
(the one without spots
that you love)
then a tiny green cricket
living among your poppies
—which you remind me, I seeded
but surely
like me
are yours

Selene's Sky

can you see
the moon tonight
where you are?

she has risen
the color of buttermilk
a waxing crescent
easing my
new moon fears

the thunder moon grows
heat domes and weatherfronts
colliding across these
not-so-united states

but we are
beneath the same
sky and stars
under Selene's
watchful eye

and for me
for tonight
that is enough

Secret Garden

I could feel tendrils of you
growing, crawling
sliding
up and across all of me
and at first I thought
you might be poet's ivy
but quickly, buds grew
small and white, pure as driven snow
suddenly bursting into bloom
and I saw a glimpse
—white lilies
and you all over
me—
before everything
faded into sunbursts
and fireworks
until all
that was left
was
us

Phoenix Rising

I feel the graveyard dirt
press against my lips
every time I dare
open my mouth
to speak

I am exhausted by
rooting for the anti-hero

I find myself stuck
in the midnights
of my discontent
haunted by ghosts
I can't seem to shake
nora and chester and dave
whispering lies
as I lie in the earth
telling me
I'm only running from
a self-fulfilling prophecy
and there are things
we can have
but not keep

and sixteen-year-old me
holds up the bottle of pills
I swallowed
then woke up
alone
no one the wiser

but the ghosts
misunderstand me

my remains buried
six feet under
the rotted pieces
cut away
excised to save
the rest of me

the transformation
from pupae to butterfly
is always glorified
but no one ever
wants to hear
of the exquisite pain
inside the chrysalis
the dissolution of self
a debt to be paid

for metamorphosis
through fire and flame
I fight to stay here
and this darkness
is not my ending

this phoenix
is rising

Wildflower Phoenix

I have never been
a rose
elegant and graceful
like our daughter
beautiful but sharp

nor am I a sunflower
tall and radiant
begging to be seen
casting shadows
on anyone
in their path

I am the ivory
peach-leaved bellflower
that lives along the path
on the edge of the drop-off
growing where I can
surviving when I must
and thriving in your garden

I am the sweet pea
you plucked and pressed

to keep forever
my petals a deep blush
always craving your touch
along my every
swell and valley

I am the wildflower
growing unattended
along the chain-link
in ditches and gutters
through cracks in the sidewalk
in riotous bloom
wherever you find me
returning to the earth
at the end of autumn
only to reseed
and grow new again
each spring
stronger and wilder
than before

Dakoda

Foxx

Reclamation

Being a woman in today's world
is challenging
Women face a lot of things
Some are seen
and others are not
A woman carries the weight
of the world on her back
and you would never notice
That's because she carries it
so effortlessly and true
Her grace gets her though
most of the things
Her joy is taking care of
her family and friends
to the end
That is her super power
and those are her kryptonite
A woman finds joy in
making sure everything is alright
She will be the hero of the night
She fights day after day
to gain her power back
This fight will be won

I am Woman

No matter what you see
I am a woman underneath
My clothes may be baggy
and my hair is short
I may walk with a strong sway
and dress in my suits
and look smoother than any cat out there.
Don't let that fool you
I am a woman underneath
I can lift almost anything you can
Take down you faster than you can blink
Don't let that fool you
I am still a hundred percent a woman underneath
I am a woman made this way by man
with strength from my heritage
wisdom from experience
I am a woman
don't forget that
no matter what you see
I am only a product of
what you made me to be

Strength

We come to build you up
what you work so hard to tear down
We come to hold the wall
before it hits the ground
We come to take back the power
of what you call right
You don't see that your way is different
from day and night
We come to rebuild
the life you say we have
We come to save you
from yourself
That is the strength we have

Happiness in Music

Music is everywhere
I enjoy the sounds that it makes
It put a pep in my step and joy in my heart
It brings back memories from the start
It relaxes my mind and helps me be free
Sometimes, it helps me find me
No ordinary tunes, just the ones that free the soul
The music that makes me move my feet
Music that makes my heart skip a beat
Music that makes me think of my love
Music that makes me cry
Music that calms my soul
Music that takes my anger away
when I'm out of control
Music that finds its way to me
is the music that brings me peace

Find Our Way Out

No chains can hold us down
for we have been held down to long
No whip can hurt us
for we have been beaten and broken down
just to be built back up
No darkness can stop us
from reaching our goal
We are the light that holds the torch
and shows the way to a brighter day
We will find a way out of the hole
you think you have us in
We will find a way out of the bondage
that you think can hold us
We are coming back to reclaim
everything you have taken from us
When we do you will find
that you didn't sit so high on that pedestal
as you thought you did
without a woman

What If

What if there was no woman to help you
What if there was no woman to guide you
What if you had to solely rely
on another man to help you
What would you do
Those late night conversation with your woman
about what to do
How things should be
You do know that all your save-the-day thoughts
came from a woman
Almost everything you do
is influenced by a woman
What would you do if you didn't have a woman
to say, *That's right, dear*
What would you do
What if women just stopped
and didn't support you anymore
Didn't give you advice
Didn't go along with your schemes
Didn't say that right
Where would you be
Believe it or not
some woman is showing you

what to do or say as we speak
Whether she's writing your speeches
Taking your notes
Working in your office
Or cooking your food
Your teachers
And the woman at the coffee shop
They all influenced you in some way
What if they were not there to help you?
Would you still be you?
You get a chance
Thank a woman because of her
You are who you are

Rise

We will rise from what you left behind
We will rise from what you tried to hide
We will rise like an eagle in the sky
We will rise to save the day
We will rise not like the others
We will rise to the highest mountains
      and deeper than the oceans
We will rise

Watch us soar

Lola

A woman who fights with all her might
A woman that is stronger than any mountain
A woman that is stronger than a diamond
A woman who is resilient in so many ways
A woman who is bold and firm
A woman with a kind heart
A woman with a caring soul
A woman with a smile that lights up a room
A woman who has essence and grace, too
A woman who will rise to the top
A woman that her beauty radiates throughout the world
A woman who is selfless and true
A woman who gives her all to many
—even when she's tired
A woman that has the courage to go on
—even after there's so many things there
to break her down

She's no ordinary woman
She's my super woman
She is my Lola Flower

Time

We have time to live and grow
Time will never stand still
It will let you keep going on and on
Time has us stunned 'cause when we try to get by
time moves faster
With everything that is going on
time will lend us a hand
Time will give us the moment we need
to get by or to hurry up fast
But time will let you know
that time is always in control

Time has no destination or no call
Time keeps us grounded with a second to count
Time waits on no one
Time can be the only one to seek
Time keeps us going even when we sleep
Time has a scheduled to keep
Time goes slow when a woman gets dressed
Time goes fast when you're having fun
Time can cause every second to be counted
We have time
So we think

Time will wait on no one
So don't take time for granted
A woman of value only takes time to grow
That time is always moving
A woman has no time to wait
Grab yours today
'Cause time doesn't wait.

Jennifer DiMarco

The Taking Tree

This skin. These bones.

These hands. This heart.

It has been forty years

of nothing more than

an ebb and flow of change.

I have won not an inch.

Gained and lost enough pounds

to grow two lives and

live more than half my own.

This mind. These dreams.

These goals. This destination.

Arriving clanless but not alone.

Forging when I thought

I would only inhabit.

Now is not the future

I was promised

but exactly the one

I anticipated.

We rarely make

the path we walk.

But we are always

the ones walking.

I remember today the child

who slept on the floor

beneath the bed

out of reach of selfish hands

out of reach of the dappled sunlight

crisscrossed window panes

like a slide puzzle to somewhere else

like a map across the hardwood.

I remember her.

She remembers me.

She sees me then

as I see me now.

Why was she never afraid?

What is fear if not a given?

This skin. These bones.

These hands. This heart.

The slow progression

toward comprehension.

The quicksilver choices

made on the bleeding edge.

The reality I know now

seeps from the wound

of a past that whispers still

through midnights

and darkling forests

from shadowed corners

and watching eyes.

This mind. These dreams.

These goals. This destination.

Those secret birds we silence

in the gilded cage of our ribs

never to sing, never to fly

lest they give themselves away.

And who then

would own me?

Half a century and more

to see my body as a tree.

Demanding so much.

Requiring so little.

Bleeding into the earth

in worship of the moon

until the tide changes

and the physical becomes

immaterial.

At last.

Of no use to them now

still I stand.

This is when

life begins.

Biographies

Michelle Lee

Michelle Lee is a Pacific Northwest native with an imagination open to possibilities. In her downtime, Michelle is an avid reader, loves to explore different areas in the northwest, speaks fluent sarcasm, and loves to bake bread. She enjoys hearing from readers and can be found on Facebook and Instagram.

Dakoda Foxx

Dakoda Foxx is a writer, actor, artist, and paralegal. She is dedicated to making a positive impact on the people she comes in contact with. She advocates for people's rights and dedicates her life to help make a change for others. She hopes her readers see that there is light at the end of any tunnel, in any situation. Dakoda's memoir, *The Magic in the Nightmare that was Me,* is a story of survival, perserverance, and a spirit that refused to be broken. She has also written a pocket-sized book in the *Haunting of Orchard House* series called *Paranoia.* Dakoda books are available at www.BlueForgePress.com. Find her on Facebook at: https://www.facebook.com/DakodaFoxxAuthorPage

Bree Indigo

Bree Indigo is a poet and songwriter. She was published in the four previous volumes of *Rise* (*Reflection, Resurrection, Revolution,* and *Recreation*), and the first six volumes of the horror anthology *Unnerving* (*Monstrosity, Descent, Eclipse, Wicked, Nightfall,* and *Phobia*), all available at www.BlueForgePress.com. Her first memoir, *Unreliable Narrator*, is forthcoming by Blue Forge Press. Indigo lives with her wife and their children in the Pacific Northwest. Find her on Instagram @bree_indigo

Jonielle McMurtrey

Jonielle McMurtrey has been writing poetry since high school. She has found writing poems as a way to connect with various souls throughout her life. She now lives in a small town in northern Arizona, after living most her life in the great northwest. Moving to Arizona was where Jonielle found much healing and self expression through the suns rays and she hopes the sun can radiate off her to brighten others lives as it has brightened hers.

Jennifer DiMarco

Winner of Bumbershoot and PNWC poetry awards, Seattle Times bestselling novelist Jennifer DiMarco first toured nationally as an author when she was nineteen years old having written novels since the age of ten. The first sixteen years of her career included the publication of contemporary drama, high fantasy, science fiction, poetry, and mystery novels as well as the production of two short films and three stage plays. During a twenty-year hiatus from prose, DiMarco married, raised two children, and worked as a filmmaker writing and directing more than a dozen feature films, half a dozen mini series, and more than a hundred short films, before returning to prose with *"Hannah at Night and Twelve Other Stories"* in 2020. DiMarco lives in the Pacific Northwest with her wife, author and actor Brianne, and their adult children, author and illustrator Maxwell, and actor and illustrator Faith. Find all of Jennifer's work at www. BlueForgePress.com

www.ingramcontent.com/pod-product-compliance
Lightning Source LLC
Chambersburg PA
CBHW061700120626
46550CB00003B/1016